Kristen and Kaleb's
BAPTISM
Adventure

A Baptism Story for Kids

Tim Adrian

Shirt-Tail Publications; Hutchinson, Kansas
ISBN: 1495204774
ISBN 13: 9781495204777
baptismadventure.com

Kristen and Kaleb's Baptism Adventure

This Book Belongs To: _____

Presented By: _____

Date: _____

Kristen and Kaleb waited with excitement in the outer office of their church. As their mother chatted with the secretary, they were wondering about their planned visit with the pastor. The church secretary explained that he was on the phone and would be able to talk in just a minute.

For the past several weeks, Kristen and Kaleb had been talking with their parents about being baptized. Matthew, their older cousin, had been baptized last summer, and they had both watched with great interest.

The place where Matthew and the others were baptized was a bit of a mystery. It was behind the platform, and the front of it was partially glass. Kristen and Kaleb could see only a few inches of water, but it was actually about as deep as the shallow end of a swimming pool.

Kristen thought about her blonde hair and how she would get it dry. Kaleb smiled as he wondered if anyone had ever put a goldfish in the water. They were both wondering where the people changed their clothes and how they actually got into the baptistery. As they thought about things like that, the door to the pastor's office opened.

The first thing Kaleb noticed about the office were several interesting items that seemed to be from other countries. Kristen looked at all the neatly arranged shelves around the room and wondered if the pastor had actually read all those books.

Both kids were quickly drawn to a small fish with wicked-looking teeth mounted on a small wooden stand. The pastor said he had gotten it as a souvenir from Brazil. "This is, or actually was, a meat-eating piranha that lived in the Amazon River," he said.

As the pastor sat behind his big desk, Kristen and Kaleb noticed pictures of his family and of baseball players. It was also the first time they had seen the pastor wearing normal clothes. They usually saw him dressed up in Sunday clothes for church.

Kristen and Kaleb almost always said hi to him on Sunday. He would usually bend over, smile, and pound knuckles or slap hands with them. Sometimes he called them Krispy and K-bub which seemed a little silly but still made them smile.

As twins, Kristen and Kaleb could almost read each other's minds, and each sensed that the other was just a little bit nervous. Maybe the pastor sensed this too, because he grinned and asked Kaleb if he had been a good boy that day. Surprised, Kaleb smirked for a moment and then confidently said, "I always am!"

Then the pastor turned to Kristen and asked, "Now tell me the truth. Has he been good today?" Kristen half chuckled and said, "Well, Pastor, he's about as good as he can be for a little brother." Their mother quickly chimed in, "She's older by only seven minutes, but, as you can tell, she likes to use that to her advantage."

The pastor said, "Well now, let's get down to business. I understand you both want to be baptized." When they both nodded their heads, he said, "Great! Let's talk about it." The twins' mom had said the pastor might ask them some questions, so they figured that was just about to happen.

Looking across the desk, the pastor said, "Kaleb, can you tell me what you know about Jesus?" Kaleb quickly thought of his Sunday School lessons and replied, "I know that He is God. And I know that He was born at Christmas. I know that He never did anything wrong."

The pastor nodded approvingly, then looked at Kristen and asked, "What do you know about His death?" This was an easy question for Kristen. "He died on the cross, and then He was buried. After three days, He rose from the grave." Kristen's mom smiled as the pastor said, "That's very good. You guys have been listening in church, haven't you?"

"Kristen," the pastor said, "Your mom tells me that you accepted Christ as your Savior several weeks ago. Can you tell me about that?" Kristen remembered the time she was saved and said, "My parents prayed with me one night. I knew Jesus would forgive me of my sins if I asked Him. I told God that I wanted Jesus as my Savior. I know that this is how people get to go to heaven."

Kaleb started talking just as the pastor looked his way. "I prayed with Mr. Chase when I was at camp last summer. It was right before bedtime, and I just wanted God to forgive my sins."

The pastor said Mr. Chase had already told him about it. Then he chuckled and said, "That Mr. Chase says *awesome* about fifteen times when he tells the story." That was no surprise to Kaleb or Kristen since it seemed that *awesome* was Mr. Chase's favorite word.

The Pastor said he was glad that both Kristen and Kaleb had accepted the Lord.

Then he began to read some verses in the Bible that told about Jesus being baptized. Kristen and Kaleb had heard the story before but enjoyed how the pastor explained it. He pointed out that when Christ was baptized, the Holy Spirit came in the form of a dove and God the Father spoke from heaven and said, "This is my beloved Son, with Him I am fully pleased." The pastor said he baptized people only in the same way that Christ was baptized, which meant they went under the water and then were brought back up.

"Some people think that baptism washes away sins," the pastor said. "But that's not true. Sins are only forgiven through faith in Christ." He added, "Baptism is important, but the way to heaven is by trusting Christ as your Savior." Both kids glanced at each other and nodded.

The pastor said the Lord wants people to follow Him in baptism. He read a Bible verse that said all people are to be baptized in the name of the Father, the Son, and the Holy Spirit. The pastor explained that baptism is an important step in following Christ.

The pastor stood and grabbed one of the pictures from the shelf behind his desk. Both kids recognized his pretty teenage daughter, Rachel. She had been a helper at Vacation Bible School last summer, and Kristen was in her group all that week. Kaleb knew her too, since she had helped lead the songs at camp.

The pastor pointed to the picture and said, "Do you know who this is?" Kristen blurted out, "Of course, it's Rachel!" He smiled and said, "Now, think about this for a minute. It's a trick question. Is this really Rachel?"

Kaleb said, "Does Rachel have a twin sister we don't know about?" When the pastor saw the puzzled look on their faces, he smiled and said, "You know this isn't really Rachel. Rachel is at home right now. This looks like her. It reminds us of her. But this is only a picture of her.

When she talks on the phone too much, I don't grab this picture, wag my finger at it, and say 'Get off the phone,' do I? No, I have to talk to the real girl."

The kids giggled a bit and the pastor continued. "Baptism is not the real thing. It's just a picture of the real thing. It reminds us of the real thing. The real thing took place long ago when Jesus died on the cross, was buried, and then rose again from the grave. When people are baptized, it's sort of like a picture of the real thing."

The pastor smiled as he said that when one little guy asked to be baptized, he got his words mixed up. He said, "Pastor, I want to get advertised." "Actually," the pastor said, "that is really not all wrong. Baptism is a way that we advertise our trust in Jesus.

When we go under the water, we are advertising our belief that Jesus died for us. When we come up out of the water, we advertise that Jesus rose from the dead for us. This is why I think people should be baptized after they have accepted Christ as their Savior."

"Why don't we go and look at the baptistery and see the changing rooms," the pastor said. Kristen, Kaleb, their mother, and the pastor walked through the church auditorium, past the platform, and through one of the back doors. This leads to a room, the pastor explained, that is used for women and girls to change into baptismal clothes.

There were four small booths in the room that reminded Kristen of restroom stalls but without toilets. The pastor pointed to robes that he said were used just for baptizing. He said most people wore a swimsuit under their robes, but sometimes people wore shorts and T-shirts. Other things in the room included towels, a mirror, and a hair dryer. Kristen felt relieved when she saw all those things.

After a minute they walked over to where the men and boys dressed. It was much like the other room but it didn't seem as fancy. The twins' mom asked if anyone else would be in the rooms, and the Pastor said that his wife usually came back to help the girls get ready and that a helper would be on the boys' side. He added, "You are welcome to help Kristen, and your husband can help Kaleb. If you would like, you can stand on the side steps of the baptistery and watch or even take pictures or a video."

Kristen and Kaleb followed the pastor several steps to the edge of the baptistery. It looked like a small swimming pool. The pastor explained that it wasn't very deep, chest high or so. He reminded them that they would go completely under the water but would be brought up again very quickly, so it wouldn't be scary at all.

From the edge of the baptistery, the pastor showed both of them how they would stand in the water and how he would stand. He showed how he wanted them to pinch their noses with one hand and then grab their wrists with the other hand. He said "As you stand like that, I will quickly lean you back into the water and then pull you forward. The whole thing will take about one second." Grinning, he added, "I call this a dry run practice," which made everyone giggle.

Kristen, Kaleb and their mother followed the pastor back through the auditorium and into the church foyer. When he didn't think the adults could hear, Kaleb whispered to Kristen, "I think I'm going to try a cannon ball when I get into the water."

In the foyer, the pastor said, "Think of baptism as 'a play'. You will play the part of Jesus. Just as Jesus was buried in the ground, you will be buried in the water. And as Jesus was raised by the power of God after three days, you will be raised out of the water. Of course, you will 'be buried' under the water only for a moment, not three full days." Kristen and Kaleb looked at each other and smiled.

Right before they left, the pastor bowed his head and said a short prayer for both Kaleb and Kristen. Their mom said, "Thank you," and as they were leaving the pastor said grinning, "Hey, K-bub! No cannon balls, OK?"

The following Sunday, both Kristen and Kaleb brought their backpacks to church. Kristen had packed her swimming suit and hair brush, along with several other things she and her mom thought she might need. She figured that Kaleb had similar items in his.

It was hard for both of them to keep still and quiet during the service, as they were so excited. Their grandparents had come to see the baptism and after church they were all going to eat at their favorite restaurant.

At the end of the service, while the church people were singing, Kristen and her mom quietly went one way, and Kaleb and his dad went another. Kaleb got ready faster because he had secretly worn his swimming suit under his pants.

Upon inspection his dad discovered an empty backpack. Kaleb's eyes widened and his mouth opened when his dad said, "Hey buddy, you don't have any dry underpants to wear home."

Soon both Kristen and Kaleb were in the warm water as the pastor began to speak to the church people. He said, "When children accept Christ; and after they understand the meaning of baptism, they should be encouraged to follow the Lord in this way."

Kaleb had volunteered to go first. The pastor said his words, and Kaleb was down and up as quick as anything. Kristen was a little nervous but remembered her mother had told her to relax and let the pastor do all the work. She grabbed her nose like the pastor had shown her, and it was over before she knew it.

As both children went back to their dressing rooms, the pastor said some things to the church people about baptism.

That afternoon, in the back of each of their Bibles, their mother wrote down the date, the name of the church, the name of the pastor and these words: Kristen and Kaleb followed the Lord in baptism.

My Own Baptism Checklist

☐ I understand Jesus is the Son of God.

☐ I understand Jesus was perfect in every way.

☐ I understand Jesus died on the cross for my sins.

☐ I understand Jesus raised from the dead after three days.

☐ I have trusted Jesus to be my Savior.

☐ I have read or heard the story of Jesus being baptized in the Bible (found in Matthew 3:13-17).

☐ I know baptism is a way that I can act out the story of Jesus.

☐ I know being baptized shows that I am a follower of Jesus.

☐ I have talked about baptism with my parent and have his/her permission.

☐ I want to be baptized!

A note to parents and teachers

Baptism should be one of the highlights in a believer's life. As mentioned in the story, it is to be a public declaration of a personal decision. Of course, it also puts into action the gospel story of Christ's death, burial, and resurrection.

It is very important children recognize that salvation and baptism are two different events. Salvation is the recognition and acceptance of God's grace, mercy, and forgiveness through Jesus Christ. So, I always ask a child to explain to me his or her understanding of how heaven is gained.

As you talk with your child about baptism, perhaps these few biblical passages will be helpful:

* The story of Christ's baptism is found in Matthew 3:13-17.
* The command for baptism is found in Matthew 28:19-20.
* An example of baptism is found in Acts 8:29-38.

It is my prayer that your child's baptism experience will be one that helps solidify in his or her heart and mind a lifelong commitment to our Lord.

May God bless.

Tim Adrian

Made in the USA
Lexington, KY
15 June 2015